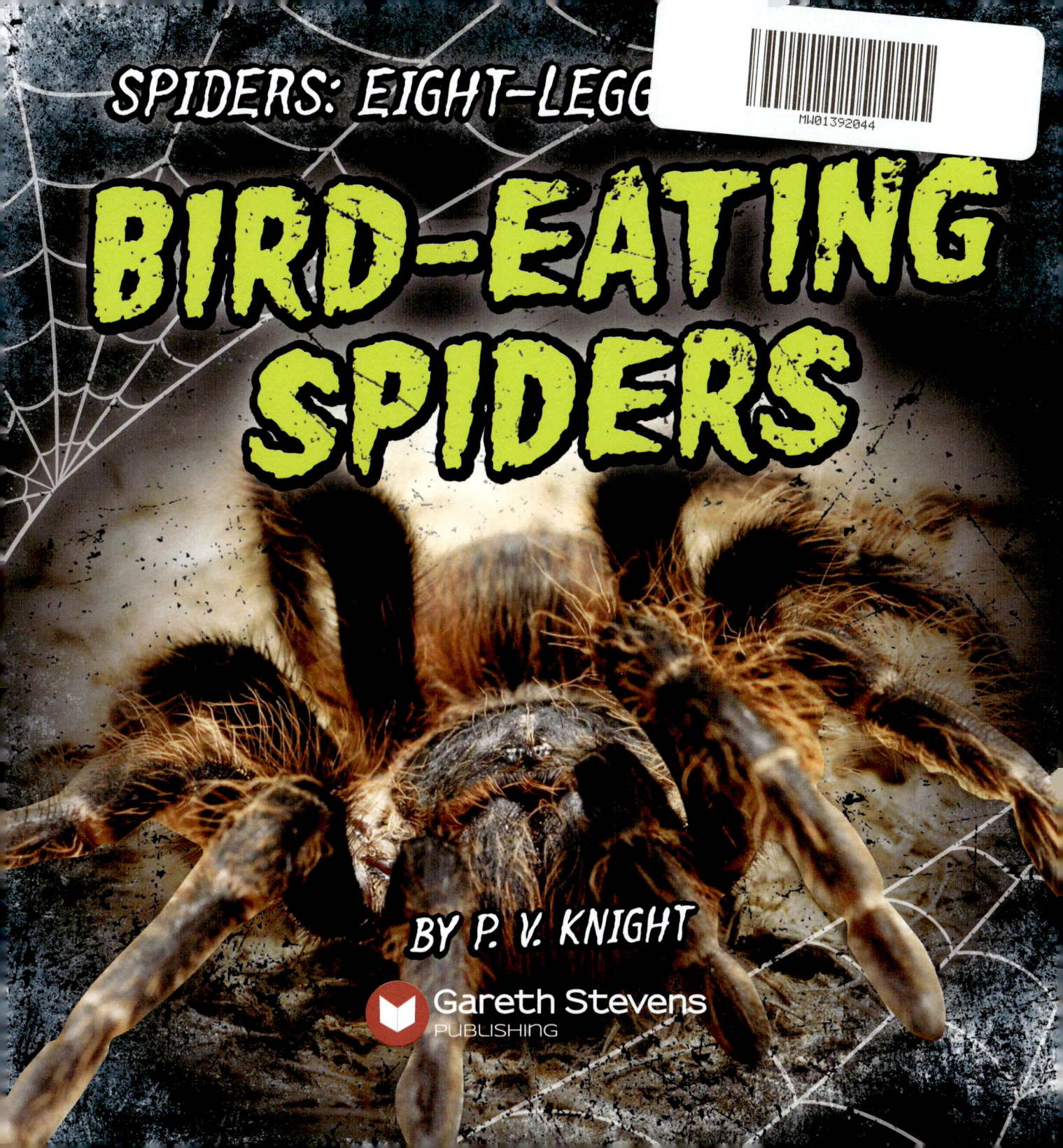

SPIDERS: EIGHT-LEGG[ED]
BIRD-EATING SPIDERS

BY P. V. KNIGHT

Gareth Stevens
PUBLISHING

Please visit our website, www.garethstevens.com. For a free color catalog of all our high-quality books, call toll free 1-800-542-2595 or fax 1-877-542-2596.

Library of Congress Cataloging-in-Publication Data

Names: Knight, P. V., author.
Title: Bird-eating spiders / P. V. Knight.
Description: New York : Gareth Stevens Publishing, [2018] | Series: Spiders, eight-legged terrors | Includes bibliographical references and index.
Identifiers: LCCN 2016056104| ISBN 9781482464849 (pbk. book) | ISBN 9781482464856 (6 pack) | ISBN 9781482464863 (library bound book)
Subjects: LCSH: Theraphosa blondi–Juvenile literature. | Tarantulas–Juvenile literature. | CYAC: Spiders.
Classification: LCC QL458.42.T5 L48 2018 | DDC 595.4/4–dc23
LC record available at https://lccn.loc.gov/2016056104

First Edition

Published in 2018 by
Gareth Stevens Publishing
111 East 14th Street, Suite 349
New York, NY 10003

Copyright © 2018 Gareth Stevens Publishing

Designer: Laura Bowen
Editor: Ryan Nagelhout

Photo credits: Cover, p. 1 (spider) Thomas Vinke/Getty Images; cover, pp. 1-24 (background) Fantom666/Shutterstock.com; cover, pp. 1-24 (black splatter) Miloje/Shutterstock.com; cover, pp. 1-24 (web) Ramona Kaulitzki/Shutterstock.com; pp. 4-24 (text boxes) Tueris/Shutterstock.com; p. 4 Glass and Nature/Shutterstock.com; p. 5 John Mitchell/Science Source/Getty Images; p. 7 BlueRingMedia/Shutterstock.com; pp. 9, 15 James H Robinson/Science Source/Getty Images; p. 11 Tim Flach/Stone/Getty Images; p. 13 (map) Pasha_Barabanov/Shutterstock.com; p. 13 (rainforest) Silvestre Garcia Ortega/Shutterstock.com; p. 17 James Gerholdt/Photolibrary/Getty Images; p. 19 Paul Miguel/Corbis Documentary/Getty Images; p. 21 Timothy Allen/Photonica World/Getty Images.

All rights reserved. No part of this book may be reproduced in any form without permission in writing from the publisher, except by a reviewer.

Printed in the United States of America

CPSIA compliance information: Batch #CS17GS: For further information contact Gareth Stevens, New York, New York at 1-800-542-2595.

CONTENTS

It Came from the Swamp! 4

As Big As a Dinner Plate 6

Deadly Hunter 8

Fierce Fighter 10

Home, Rainy Home 12

Spider Beginnings 14

Growing Up 16

Friend or Foe? 18

Dangers Ahead 20

Glossary 22

For More Information 23

Index 24

Words in the glossary appear in **bold** type the first time they are used in the text.

IT CAME FROM THE SWAMP!

This creature makes its home in **swamps** deep in South American **rainforests**. It's huge for its kind. It's covered with hair and creeps about on eight legs. It uses **venom** to overcome its **prey**.

What is this scary-sounding creature? It's the goliath, or giant, bird-eating spider! It belongs to a group of large, hairy spiders called tarantulas. Because of their appearance, many people find tarantulas quite terrifying. But are they really? Learn more if you dare!

TERRIFYING TRUTHS

The goliath bird-eating spider was named by European explorers who witnessed this tarantula eating a hummingbird!

This unlucky young bird has become the prey of a goliath bird-eating spider.

AS BIG AS A DINNER PLATE

The goliath bird-eating spider is the world's second-largest spider. With its legs spread out, it's 12 inches (30 cm) across—the size of a dinner plate! It weighs up to 6 ounces (175 g). That's equal to about 30 quarters!

The spider has two main body parts: the cephalothorax (seh-fuh-luh-THOHR-aks), which combines the head and **thorax**, and the abdomen, or stomach. At the end of the abdomen, parts called spinnerets produce silk. Even with eight eyes, its eyesight is poor. A hard exoskeleton, or shell, covers its body.

TERRIFYING TRUTHS

The goliath bird-eating spider uses fangs to put venom into its prey. Its fangs are about an inch (2.5 cm) long!

PARTS OF A GOLIATH BIRD-EATING SPIDER

spinneret

eyes

fang

leg

abdomen

cephalothorax

This shows the parts of a goliath bird-eating spider—and all spiders!

DEADLY HUNTER

Although the goliath bird-eating spider makes silk, it doesn't spin webs to catch prey. So how does it catch its food? It knows when a creature is nearby because the hairs covering its body sense the smallest movements and **vibrations** in the air around it. Then it leaps suddenly and sinks its fangs into its prey! The venom **paralyzes** the prey, and the spider has a meal.

The goliath bird-eating spider eats bugs, frogs, small snakes, lizards, and other small animals. In spite of its name, it almost never eats birds!

TERRIFYING TRUTHS

The goliath bird-eating spider has a straw-like mouth with no teeth. Its fangs put juices into its prey that turn the prey's insides into liquid, so the spider can suck up its meal!

These are the huge, terrifying fangs the goliath bird-eating spider uses to paralyze its prey.

FIERCE FIGHTER

When in danger, the goliath bird-eating spider has many ways to fight an enemy. It may try to scare the creature off by rubbing together stiff hairs on its legs. This is called stridulation (strih-juh-LAY-shun). It makes a hissing noise loud enough to be heard 15 feet (4.6 m) away!

The spider can also shoot tiny hairs from its abdomen. These hairs stick in the enemy's skin and are highly **irritating**. The spider may also rear up on its back legs to display its terrible fangs.

TERRIFYING TRUTHS

How irritating are the abdominal hairs of the goliath bird-eating spider? Small animals such as mice can die from the irritation!

This goliath bird-eating spider has reared up on its back legs to let its enemy get a good look at its long fangs.

11

HOME, RAINY HOME

The goliath bird-eating spider lives in the rainforests found in the South American countries of Venezuela, Guyana, Suriname, French Guiana, and Brazil. It prefers to live deep in the rainforest, in the very drippiest, wettest parts, such as swamps. Yuck!

The spider usually makes its home in a burrow, or hole in the ground, that it lines with silk. It may dig its own burrow or take over one deserted by another animal. Sometimes it lives under a rock or a fallen log.

TERRIFYING TRUTHS

Several other tarantulas are also known as bird-eating spiders. They're found around the world—not only in Brazil and Central America, but also in China and Australia.

WHERE GOLIATH BIRD-EATING SPIDERS LIVE

Venezuela
Guyana
Suriname
French Guiana
Brazil

South America

This map shows the places where the goliath bird-eating spider is at home.

▨ goliath bird-eating spider range

Amazon rainforest in South America

13

SPIDER BEGINNINGS

Like all spiders, the goliath bird-eating spider starts life as an egg. The female lays 50 to 150 eggs in a large silk sack after **mating** with a male. She stores it in her burrow and guards it to keep it safe.

The babies, called spiderlings, come out of the eggs after about 2 months. They stay in their mother's burrow until they molt, or cast off their exoskeleton, for the first time. Then they leave and begin life on their own.

TERRIFYING TRUTHS

The female may add irritating hairs from her abdomen to the silk sack around her eggs. This keeps the eggs safe from flies that would harm them.

This goliath bird-eating spider guards the entrance to its burrow. Perhaps it is a female, with eggs or spiderlings inside the burrow.

GROWING UP

The spiderlings molt many times as they grow into adults. It takes them 2 to 3 years to become adults. They continue to molt after they're grown. Because there's new growth every time they molt, they're able to grow a new leg if they've lost one!

Female goliath bird-eating spiders can live up to 20 years. Males usually live only 3 to 6 years. Why is that? About half of all males are killed or hurt by females while trying to mate!

TERRIFYING TRUTHS

After a goliath bird-eating spider molts, it's soft and rubbery. It takes several days for the new exoskeleton to harden. Small bugs can easily kill the spider during this time.

This young goliath bird-eating spider rests next to its recently cast off old exoskeleton. It must now wait for its new exoskeleton to harden.

FRIEND OR FOE?

As scary as the goliath bird-eating spider looks and sounds, it's not a serious danger to people. It will only attack if it feels it's in danger. And most people say a bite is no worse than a wasp sting. Sometimes, however, it causes a lot of pain and makes you sick to your stomach.

Those irritating hairs the spider shoots from its abdomen can cause real problems if they get around your eyes and mouth. The way to avoid these problems is simple: Don't bother the spiders!

TERRIFYING TRUTHS

Like all spiders, the goliath bird-eating spider helps people by keeping the bug population under control.

This pinkfoot goliath bird-eating spider looks fierce indeed when seen so close. But remember: It doesn't want to hurt you, and it helps keep pests under control.

DANGERS AHEAD

The goliath bird-eating spider faces more danger from people than people face from it. People capture wild spiders to sell as pets. They're also destroying the spiders' rainforest homes. People use **chemicals** to kill bug pests the spiders like to eat, and the spiders suffer harm from those chemicals. And some people in South America find the spider very tasty when it's roasted over a fire!

The goliath bird-eating spider is an amazing creature that actually helps people. We need to keep this spider safe!

TERRIFYING TRUTHS

Perhaps as many as nine out of every 10 spiders caught to be pets die before they can be sold.

These children in Venezuela are roasting goliath bird-eating spiders they've caught in the forest near their village. Yum!

21

GLOSSARY

chemical: matter that can be mixed with other matter to cause changes

fang: a hard, sharp-pointed body part a spider uses to put venom in its prey

irritating: causing a stinging feeling

mate: to come together to produce babies

paralyze: to make unable to move

prey: an animal hunted by other animals for food

rainforest: a forest that gets at least 100 inches (254 cm) of rain each year

swamp: wet, spongy land that has trees and is covered by water at least part of the year

thorax: the part of the body between the head and the abdomen

venom: poison made in an animal's body and put into its prey by biting or stinging

vibration: a very fast movement back and forth

FOR MORE INFORMATION

BOOKS

Archer, Claire. *Bird-Eating Spiders*. Minneapolis, MN: Abdo Kids, 2015.

Britton, Tamara L. *Bird-Eating Spiders*. Edina, MN: ABDO Publishing, 2011.

Meinking, Mary. *Tarantula vs. Bird*. Chicago, IL: Raintree, 2011.

WEBSITES

Goliath Bird-Eating Spider
aboutanimals.com/arachnid/goliath-bird-eating-spider/
Enjoy some awesome photos, and read a full account of goliath bird-eating spiders on this site.

Tarantula
animals.sandiegozoo.org/animals/tarantula
Learn about tarantulas in general on this San Diego Zoo website.

World's Largest Spider
video.nationalgeographic.com/video/tarantula_goliath
Watch a goliath bird-eating spider in action, and read more about it on this website.

Publisher's note to educators and parents: Our editors have carefully reviewed these websites to ensure that they are suitable for students. Many websites change frequently, however, and we cannot guarantee that a site's future contents will continue to meet our high standards of quality and educational value. Be advised that students should be closely supervised whenever they access the Internet.

INDEX

abdomen 6, 10, 14, 18

burrow 12, 14, 15

cephalothorax 6

chemicals 20

eggs 14, 15

exoskeleton 6, 14, 16, 17

eyes 6

fangs 6, 8, 9, 10, 11

female 14, 16

hairs 8, 10, 14, 18

males 16

pets 20

prey 4, 5, 6, 8, 9

rainforests 4, 12, 20

silk 6, 8, 12

silk sack 14

South America 4, 12, 20

spiderlings 14, 15, 16

spinnerets 6

straw-like mouth 8

stridulation 10

swamps 4, 12

tarantulas 4, 12

venom 4, 6, 8